I0015008

Learn Python

*Crash Course to Learn Algorithms
Just By Doing Some Practice. It Will
Really Help Your Career Out*

TIM WIRED

Table of Contents

Introduction

Congratulations on purchasing *Learn Python* and thank you for doing so.

We are going to spend some time taking a look at how to work not only with the Python language, and how we are able to use this to handle some of our machine learning and the different algorithms that we are able to do with this if your business is going to handle some of the work with data science as well. There are a lot of options and benefits of working with this data science, and handling this whole process is going to be difficult in some situations as well. This guidebook is going to spend some time working with data science, and how Python is going to work to help us get the algorithms done and seeing the patterns and insights that are found inside of that data as well.

There are a lot of different parts that happen with data science and Python that we are to handle when it comes to our business. We will start out with a simple look at the Python language, how to work with the benefits of Python, and so much more.

After we will look at some of the work that we are able to do with machine learning. Machine learning is going to be some of the backbones that we are able to look at when it is time to handle all of the different data that we are able to work with to improve our business. Understanding how this works, and how it can combine with Python in order to work with the algorithms will be discussed later in this guidebook as well. Along with learning some of the information that we need about machine learning, we will also take a look at some of the different ways that we can work with machine learning and more.

Then we get to some of the meat and potatoes that we are able to see when it comes to working with machine learning and Python. There are so many great algorithms that you are able to focus on when it is time to work with the data that you have, and it really depends on what kind of data you are working with, what information you would like to find out of all that, and what we hope to accomplish out of all this as well.

This guidebook will go more into some of the algorithms that you are able to work with along the way as well. We will look at how to handle the decision trees and random forests, neural networks, support vector machines, clustering, KNN, and so much more. This is going to help us to really understand how to work with machine learning and how to pick out the right option that we are able to work with when it is time to start with our own algorithms as well.

There is so much that we are able to work with the Python language, especially when we want to work with machine learning and creating some of the algorithms and more that we would like to handle. If you have been looking at data science and hoping to make it work for some of the things that you want to do like understanding your customer, learning more about the industry, and beating your competition, you will find that this is going to be one of the best methods to help you to get more out of the process as well. When you are ready to get started with the process of data science and machine learning from Python, make sure to check out this guidebook to help you get started.

There are plenty of books on this subject on the market, thanks again for choosing this one! Every effort was made to ensure it is full of as much useful information as possible, please enjoy it!

Chapter 1: What is the Python Language?

Before we get a chance to go more into machine learning and all that this cool technology is able to do for us, we first need to take a closer look at some of the coding that is going to happen behind the scenes with this language. There are so many algorithms and other parts of the process that go on behind the scenes here that it is important for us to take some time to learn about them. This is so we can get a more accurate view of what is happening in Python.

The language that we are going to focus on when it is time to handle machine learning is the Python language. There may be a lot of different options that we are able to focus on when we want to do some machine learning. You will find that the Python language is going to be one of the best options to work with. There are a ton of benefits that come with the Python language, and that is one of the main reasons why we will want to choose this option over some of the others.

This chapter is going to spend some time taking a look at the benefits of Python and all of the reasons why it is going to provide us with some of the results that we want when it comes to machine learning and some of the algorithms that we want to focus on here. Python is one of the best options that we are able to use to get this done because of all the great features, and as we go through this guidebook, we will see more about how we are able to use this for our needs.

You are more than likely excited to get into some of the work that can happen with machine learning and some of the algorithms that we will talk about in a bit. But before we are able to get to that point and start using this for our needs, we need to learn more about the Python language. Some of the different parts of the Python language that we need to learn and explore before combining it together with machine learning and data science includes:

Python Programming Language

Easy — Popular
Useful — General Purpose
Powerful — Large Libraries

How to Work with the Python Language

If you are interested in working with Python, there are going to be a few basic concepts that we need to focus on ahead of time to make sure that we are able to use this language in the manner that we would like. First, we have to understand that Python is a language that does not need to rely on compiling to get the results that it needs. Python is going to be a language that is interpreted. This means that you are able to run the program as soon as you make some changes to the file. This is a nice thing because it is going to make things like iterating, revising, and troubleshooting the program much faster than what you will see with some of the other languages out there.

As you will quickly see when you work with the Python language, this is actually one of the easier ones to code in. Even as someone who has not spent a lot of time working with Python, and you haven't been able to do any coding in the past, you will find that it is easy enough to learn, and you can easily have a basic program up and running and ready to go in just a few minutes when working on this option.

As you get onto the Python language, assuming that you already have it downloaded and installed on your computer, it is a good idea to spend some time messing around and learning about the interpreter. You are able to use this interpreter from Python to test out some of the code that you have, without having to add it to the program to do this. This is going to be one of the best ways for a beginner to learn more about how a specific command is going to work, or it can allow you to write away a program that you would like to just practice with before throwing out.

We can also work with this in order to learn a bit about how Python is able to handle some of the variables and objects that are found in your codes. Python is unique in that it is considered one of the object-oriented languages, or OOP. This means that all of the parts that show up in the program are going to be treated as objects.

Along the same line, you will not need to go through and declare the variables that you are doing at the beginning of the program because you are able to do this at any time that is the easiest for your coding instead. This one also doesn't require that you go through and specify the type of variable that you are using, so it will not matter if you are working with a string, integer, or not, because the compiler will be able to figure this all out for you.

These are just a few of the parts that we need to know more about when it comes to handling the Python language. This is a really great language to work with, and it comes with a ton of intricate parts that have to work together in a strong manner in order to see some of the success that we would like. When we are able to put all of these parts together and learn how to make them work, you will find that it is easier than ever to really write out some of the codes that we want, even within the Python language.

The Benefits of Python

When it comes to picking out a coding language, you will find that there are a lot of benefits that will come from using Python, and many reasons why you are able to use this coding language rather than some of the others that are out there. This language is simple to learn and perfect for someone who is just getting started with coding, to make sure that they are able to get their coding done in the manner that they would like.

In fact, the Python language has been designed in order to make it easier for some of the coding that we want to do, even as a beginner. It is written out in the English language, and some of the codes that come with it are simple enough to make life a little bit easier. Even if you have never gone through and done any coding at all, you will find that this language is going to be easier to handle even for you as a beginner.

Even though this is going to be a coding language that is meant to help us as a beginner, it still has some of the power that you need in order to get the coding done. Even when it comes to machine learning and some of the harder parts that we need with the different algorithms that show up throughout this guidebook, you will find that we are able to use Python to get it all done. There are some of those who are going to be worried about Python being too easy for them to work with some of the more complex things that they want to have along the way, but as we take a look at how this language actually works and what we are able to do with it, you will find that it is able to handle any of the different things that you would like along the way, no matter how simple or complex they may be.

This is just the start of the benefits that we are able to see when it comes to working with the Python language. There are quite a few benefits that we are able to focus on as well, and these are going to include options like:

1. A large community that we are able to work with and enjoy. One thing that a lot of people who are starting out

with machine learning are going to really like about this process is that there is such a large community that they are able to work with. This helps them to find the right answers when they have questions or concerns, or when there is something that is just not working out for them. This community is going to include a lot of programmers of all different types of degrees of knowledge including those who have been coding for a long time, those who are newer, and some that are in between. This is a great resource for you to use to get the results that you want in the process.

2. Lots of libraries and extensions that you are able to utilize. As you get into some of the work that you want to do with the Python language, you will find that it is going to be a great option to help you to get your done with python overall. There are libraries to help you with machine learning, deep learning, artificial intelligence, math, science, and so much more in the process.

3. I can work with machine learning. One of the biggest reasons that a lot of programmers like to learn more about the Python language is because it is going to be able to work well with machine learning. Machine learning is a big thing for a lot of businesses as it helps them to reach their customers and basically sorts

through large amounts of data for them in less time. Since Python can be used to handle and even run some of the algorithms that are critical to machine learning, we can see how the two go hand in hand, and why so many people and companies want to learn how to use this for their own needs as well.

4. It is considered an OOP language to make things easier: OOP languages, or object programming languages, are going to be those that can help us to keep the code organized with the help of classes and objects. We are able to create the classes that we want, and they work as boxes to hold onto the various objects that show up in our code as well. This is basically a method that we are able to use that keeps things organized and ensures that we are able to take care of all the parts that we need in our code, without any of the headaches that may have been more prevalent in the older coding languages.

5. It can provide us with the options to combine together with some of the other languages that you need to get the job done. Sometimes, especially when we are working with some of the things that we want to get done in machine learning, we will find that we will need to work with another language other than Python to make it happen. The neat thing is that we are able to use some of

the libraries that work well with Python, such as TensorFlow, to write out the codes that we want in Python, and then the library will go back and convert it into another language to execute it the way that we would like. It is that simple.

    a. This is a great feature that we are able to enjoy when it comes to working with Python and getting it to do some of the work that we would like along the way. You can combine some of the ease of use of Python with some of the other languages out there and find that it provides you all of the benefits that you are looking for.

There are a lot of different options that we are able to work with when it comes to the Python language. This language has a lot that we are able to use when it comes to creating this kind of program and will really help us to see some of the results that we need when it comes to handling all of our coding needs. There may be other coding languages that we are able to work with, but none of them are going to provide us with the power, versatility, and ease of use that we are able to get with Python. And with that in mind, we are going to spend some time through this guidebook looking at what Python is all about, and how we are able to use it to help us get some of our work done in machine learning as well.

Chapter 2: Understanding the World of Machine Learning

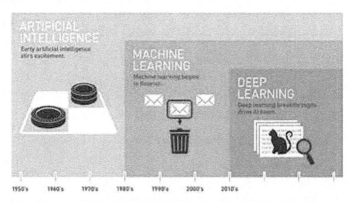

Now that we know a little bit more about the Python language and all of the things that we are able to do with that language to make our work easier to handle, it is time for us to enter into the world of machine learning as well. There are a lot of different parts that come with machine learning, and it is going to help our business to gain a good advantage and get ahead of the competition as well. To keep it simple for now though (we will take a look at some of the algorithms that we are able to use with this one later on), we are going to focus our attention on understanding the world of machine learning and how it is going to work to train our systems and our computers.

To start, machine learning is basically going to be a process that helps us, through the use of a variety of algorithms, to properly train some of our systems to make decisions on their own. With the right algorithms in place, we are able to go through and really make sure that our systems and more will behave in the manner that we want and that they will be able to interact with the other people who use them as well.

This is just a basic summary of what we are going to see with machine learning, and this chapter is going to spend some more time going through it and learning how we are able to make this work for some of our needs as well. Some of the different parts of machine learning that we need to take some time to explore now will include:

What is Machine Learning?
The first thing that we need to take a look at is the basics of machine learning. To keep it simple, we will find that machine learning is going to be the application of artificial intelligence that is going to offer our machines and systems the ability to learn and act in a manner that is similar to humans, without us having to program them on our own. This process of learning is something that can get better and improve over time and is going to happen when we feed new information and data into the machine, and even when the system gets to have interactions and observations with the real-world through use of that particular program run by machine learning.

When we are working with a system of machine learning, there are going to be three main components that we need to spend some of our time on. These will include the model, parameters, and also the learner. Let's start at the beginning of the model. This model is going to be the system that is in place that can help us to make predictions or identifications. If we have the right model in place, it is easier to go through all of that information and really find the insights and predictions that we need.

From there, we are able to focus on some of the parameters that are found in a machine learning system. These are unique because they are going to be any of the signals or factors that the model is going to use in order to form the decisions that it makes. And then there is a learner, which is going to be any of the systems that will be able to adjust the model, usually by making some adjustments to the parameters by observing the differences in the predictions versus the actual outcome that we want.

The working of any machine learning system is going, to begin with, to help the model. In the beginning, you will need to give the model a prediction to the system. The model is going to depend on these parameters being in place before it is able to make any of the calculations that we need. The system of machine learning is then going to be able to use its own mathematical equation to help express the parameters and to efficiently form a trend line of what it should actually do.

So, the real-life information is going to be entered as soon as that model is set. For the most part, the real score is not going to match up with the model. Some of these are going to be above, and sometimes, we will see some show up below the predicted line that is there. And this is where some of the learning components that we want to see with machine learning is going to get started.

This information that we are able to provide to the system of machine learning is going to be known as our training data. This training data is important because the learner can utilize it to train itself so that the model learns how to behave and gets better at the work that it is doing. The learner is then going to observe the scores and determine the difference between what the model is getting and the actual results that it should get. Then it is able to use some math in order to adjust some of the assumptions that were initially made. Now, with the new set of scores and some of the adjustments that were run along the way, we will be able to run through the system again.

After this, the comparison is going to happen and will be completed between the revised model that the learner just came up with, and the real score as well. If it is successful, the scores are going to be at least a little bit closer to the prediction in this option than they were in the first place. However, this doesn't mean that they are going to be ideal. We do need to go through this process a few times in order to help make sure that the system gets as accurate as possible.

So, after this second round, the parameters will need to be adjusted again so that the learner is able to reshape their model again. You will have to work through the comparisons over and over again until the model is able to predict the outcome in an accurate manner.

This system of machine learning is going to make adjustments again and again in this kind of manner, at least until things get right. This is going to be something that is known as gradient learning or gradient descent. And while this is a process that can take some time and may not be as easy to work with as we might hope, you will find that it is a good way to take a look at how this kind of system is able to learn and get better at the job that it should do.

What Can Machine Learning Be Used For?

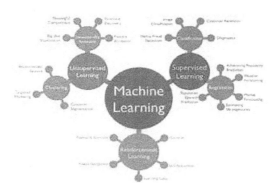

The next thing that we are able to take a look at here is some of the ways that we are able to use machine learning for some of our needs. Machine learning is going to be usable in a lot of different sectors, and the uses of this kind of language are likely to grow over time, as we develop new and exciting ways that we can work with it as well. Some of the sectors that are able to work with machine learning will include:

1. We will find that machine learning is going to have a lot of applications that we are able to enjoy whether we are working with the healthcare world, retail, publishing, and so many other industries.
2. Google and Facebook are going to work with machine learning in order to help push the relevant kind of advertisements based on the behaviors of the searching for that user in the past.
3. Machine learning is also able to handle some multi-dimensional and multi-variety data inside of some dynamic environment.
4. Machine learning is going to enable us to have the efficient utilization and time cycle reduction of all the resources that you have.
5. When we take a look at data entry, machine learning is able to help us simplify some of the documentation that tends to take a lot of time in the first place.
6. Machine learning is going to help us to improve some of the precision that we are going to see in the models and rules in the world of finances.

7. Machine learning is also going to help detect spam in emails and messages.

8. Machine learning is going to allow us to have an appropriate lifetime value prediction and can make it easier for us to segment the customers better than before.

9. Machine learning is going to assist when it comes to accurately forecasting sales and can make marketing for our products so much easier overall.

Machine Learning vs. Artificial Intelligence

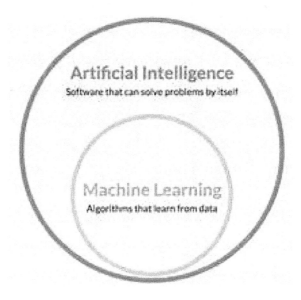

Another thing that we need to get started with is how machine learning and artificial intelligence are going to work. Both of these are going to be used interchangeably in many cases, especially when it comes to big data. But we have to learn that these are not going to be the same things, and we need to be able to see some of the differences that come with them.

To start with, artificial intelligence is going to be a branch that is found inside of computer science and can be defined as the ability of a machine or a computer program to help learn from experience and will perform tasks in the same way as humans. We can now take a look at the differences between machine learning and artificial intelligence in the information that is below.

First, we can take a closer look at artificial intelligence. This is going to be a broader concept that is going to address the use of machines to perform the tasks that are considered smart. The goal here is to enhance the chances of success, but it does not ensure that there is accuracy. In addition, AI is going to be a higher cognitive process, and it is going to function more like a computer program that is going to perform smart work. This helps to lead to wisdom or intelligence. In addition, we are going to see that it involves the creation of a system that is able to mimic the behavior of humans.

Then we are able to take a look at machine learning. This is going to be one of the applications of artificial intelligence, and it is going to be based on the idea of giving machine access to data that it needs and allowing them to learn for themselves. The goal is to enhance the accuracy, but it doesn't care about success. Machine learning enables the system to learn from the data.

Another thing to look at is that machine learning is going to be a simple concept where a machine is able to take the data and then learn from it. Machine learning is always a good thing because it is going to lead to more knowledge. Machine learning is then going to lead to the creation of algorithms that are self-learning.

The Different Types of Machine Learning

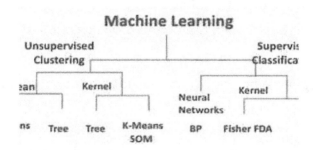

To help us to break down some of the real problems that we have with this work, and to make sure that we have a machine learning system that is able to tackle it all, we need to get to know more about the algorithms types that come with machine learning. There are our main types of algorithms that we are able to work with, and often it depends on the kind of work that we want to do with them to help us choose which one to pick. The four main types of learning algorithms that we are able to work with are going to include:

1. Supervised
2. Unsupervised
3. Semi-supervised
4. Reinforcement

First, we are able to take a look at the kind that is known as supervised machine learning. These are going to be the ones that will contain a target or an outcome variable, and sometimes a dependent variable, which is going to be predicted from the set of independent variables that we give to it. A function that is able to map out the inputs to the desired outputs can be generated while doing these variables as well.

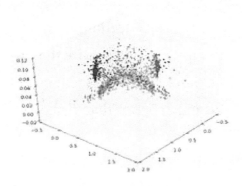

Basically, these kinds of algorithms are going to take a lot of examples that they can hold onto and will learn from those. We need to make sure that we have a lot of labeled data to make this work though. The algorithm is able to take the information that it is provided, look over the input and the corresponding output, and then figure out how to use this new knowledge to their advantage in order to make good predictions about new data that the algorithm sees in the future.

The second type of learning algorithm that we are able to work with is going to be the unsupervised machine learning. This is the one that we are going to work with when we don't have an outcome of some kind of target variable for helping us to estimate or make some of the predictions that you need. So, you will find that with this one we are not going to tell the system where we would like it to go.

Instead, our system is going to need to learn how to understand where to go and what answers to give from the data that we provide to it in the first place. This is going to happen when the algorithms are able to utilize techniques that will input data to detect patterns, groups, and summarize the points of data, mine for rules, and even describe the data to those who want to use it in a manner that is much better than before.

The algorithms that come with this one are going to be used mainly to help out with pattern detection and descriptive modeling. These algorithms are going to be used in many cases where human experts are not going to know what to look for in the data. There are a lot of algorithms that come with this will include the Apriori algorithm, K-means, and more.

The third option that we need to work with is going to be known as semi-supervised machine learning. In the other two types of algorithms, either the label is going to be there for the observations, or there are not going to be variables for all of the different observations that we want to use. This kind of learning is going to fall kind of in the middle of supervised and unsupervised learning that we talked about already. This is because it is going to rely on both labeled data and unlabeled data.

You will find that with the semi-supervised type of learning, accuracy is going to be improved quite a bit because we are able to use a small amount of data that is labeled along with some of the unlabeled data to help us train the work that we need to get done. There are quite a few options that you are able to use in order to help get this kind of learning done.

The final option that we are able to focus our attention on is going to be known as reinforcement machine learning. This is going to be the kind where we are not going to have any sets of data that are labeled or unlabeled, so it is not going to be like the other options that we talked about before. It is going to work in a way that will have the machine live in an environment of trial and error, and the machine is able to learn in this manner.

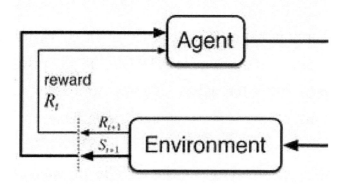

The machine that has some reinforcement algorithms working on it is going to be trained in order to make some business decisions that are accurate by learning from the experiences that it has had in the past, and then capturing the best knowledge that its possible knowledge. This kind of learning is going to be powerful but more complex than some of the other options, and it is going to help us to get a lot of cool things done with the work that we want to do as well.

There are so many ways that you are able to work with machine learning and ensure that it is going to do some of the work that you would like along the way. Learning more about how this can work and what we are able to do with it is going to make a world of difference in the way that we can handle some of the data science that we want to accomplish, and how we can make sure that the computer is going to learn in the manner that we would like.

Many businesses like to work with machine learning because they like all that this is able to do for them, and all of the benefits that they are able to get along the way as well. Machine learning can make it possible to learn from a lot of data that you have collected, in a manner that is faster and more efficient than what we are able to do manually. These predictions and insights can help us to make better decisions that propel our businesses forward and will ensure that we are going to see some of the best results for this in the process as well.

We will explore through this guidebook some of the many great things that you are able to do when it comes to working with machine learning, especially when you talk about how it works with the Python language. And we will look at some of the neat things that we are able to do when it is time to handle these algorithms, in all of the categories that we talked about before. This will help us to really learn more about how we can use machine learning to further our business.

Chapter 3: What are These Algorithms Used For?

As many products that work with machine learning start to grow and will continue to target enterprise throughout the world, you will find that these products are going to start to make a divergence into two channels. The first one is going to be the products that are going to become increasingly meta in order to make sure that machine learning itself is going to do better with its own predictive capacity. And then we are going to end up with those that are going to be more granular in their focus by addressing some of the specific problems that the verticals are going to experience sometimes.

And while the latest type of products in machine learning through both of these channels can reduce some of the points of pain in data science, especially for those that are used in a more business environment, there are some experts that warn that machine learning, no matter how much it grows, is not going to be able to solve two main issues, no matter the predictive capacity of these tools. These include:

1. Solving some of the unique problems for a particular business use case.

2. Cleaning up the data that you are using in the first place so that it is actually valuable in the workflow that is needed with machine learning.

A Look to Begin

When we first hear about machine learning and the term artificial intelligence, these are often going to be mistaken for some of the technologies that are out there that we think can replace people. Computers will find people, sell them the things that they want and need, and then there is no need any longer to have a human work in marketing, for example.

However, as more of this technology comes out, and it becomes a bigger part of or lives, it turns out that these technologies are still going to need some human interaction and help in order to get things done. They are not able to replace our jobs and the work that we are able to do, no matter how strong or powerful they may seem when we first get started.

Computers can do some of the grunge work there, but only humans are able to really take the information, see what matters the most, and then use it. Marketers and other fields are not going to be replaced with this automation and the user of machine learning, but they will find that using it can be in their best interest and can help them to complete their job in a more effective manner.

The first thing that we are able to look at here is how to take note of what machine learning is able to do, and where it is going to lack. You are able to program it in a manner to help seek out attributes and even count how many clicks we are going to be able to get on a particular website. This can be great news because it helps us to really learn from the data that we have for a long time to come.

Machine learning is even able to take this a bit further by recognizing the subject lines of a campaign. It can help us to tag images when we are doing a visual search, it can analyze the sentences that it sees, and undertake some decision-making in real-time, do power recommendation engines, and even engage in bidding that happens in the real world.

These are some of the amazing things that we are going to see when it comes to artificial intelligence or machine learning. Both of these are going to be best applied either when there is going to be a large surplus of the consumer or when you are in a business process that is more low yield than others. While there are a lot of functions that we are able to work with the help of machine learning, you will find that there are some places where it is going to be lacking as well. And we will be able to look through some of those in this chapter as well.

For example, we should not waste our time trying to apply machine learning and all that it is able to do to tasks where humans are already able to do them in an effective manner. This would be something like air traffic control when we are in an airport. If there is already a task that is pretty optimized overall, incorporating some machine learning into it would not really serve any purpose, and it would definitely not provide us with a good return on investment for our time either. By learning, we will find that AI, and the processes that come with machine learning, can become smarter in the process.

We have already seen that machine learning and artificial intelligence are found across the entirety of marketing and sales. And this is just one of the places that we are able to use this kind of technology. The more that we spend our time learning how to work through this, the more uses we are going to find with this kind of process as well.

Avoiding Error

Before machine learning is as effective as we want, the machine has to be able to learn. Programmers are often going to shovel a lot of data, terabytes, or more into the hopper, all gladly digested by the learning algorithm that they chose. Ironically though, the system is no less human than those who are building it all up. This means that there will be some errors lurking if we are not careful and if we just throw all of the information together without spending time on it along the way. We need to make sure that we screen it out along the way as well.

We can take a look at an example of this with Lattice Engines. This is a solution that will look for patterns in the data in order to identify who is likely to convert to a sale. According to this company, they use about 8 percent of the data just to train the model that they are working with. Then the rest of it is going to be set aside to use in testing the model, which is something that we need to do with all of our products. This extra 20 percent is going to be used in order to test the model to see if it is able to make some accurate predictions. This is done because the answer is already known, and we can check to see how well this process is going to work along the way.

If machine learning is considered king in the industry, then data is going to be the queen in this relationship. If you don't have enough or rich training data, then no algorithm for machine learning is going to do the job, no matter how good it is. The best way to make sure that you are picking out data that is higher in quality and works for the programming that you are doing is to use more data. Often confidence in your data is going to come when we are able to get a different perspective on the same data but from different sources. If a lot of sources end up agreeing, then we know that the data is more likely to be true as well.

For many situations, the data, especially the analysis, and other solutions will be used by many companies right now. Data is going to be used in order to help out with the training, and then we are able to measure the validation, improve the model that we have, and understand the differences that we need to address as well. This also needs to have an extra layer to help us to remove some of the outliers. If we find that there is something that is not right with the data, then things are going to end up suffering from the algorithm that we are working with.

Remember here that quality is not going to be guaranteed all of the time, but quantity is something that can help us to make up for all of this. With data sets that are smaller, the impact of some of the bad data is going to be so much worse as well. Whenever we see that someone is failing, it is often because the set of data that they worked with was too small.

Keep the Programmers in the Loop

Another thing that we need to remember when we are working with this is that machine learning should not be something that we put on autopilot. Instead, it is going to be the co-pilot in the projects that we are working with. We need to have a person there who is able to make some good judgment calls on the output that the machine is able to provide to us.

Machine learning is able to do a lot of really cool things, but it is also still a relatively new technology, and there is still room to find some error. There are a few methods that we are able to use in order to put some constraints on the problem. All AI systems should take the feedback from humans or the overrides, and then can provide some justification for some of the actions. The transparency of the AI actions is going to be an absolute requirement for building up some trust with the users that we have.

Machine learning is able to do some of the programming tasks that we need that are not really possible for humans. For example, it is able to go through a year or more of data and see what is inside of it in just a few minutes. But then there are things that humans are able to do that may not seem possible for a machine. Does the pattern spotted by a machine seem to make sense for what is going on? Or does it end up being something more like an anomaly and doesn't make a lot of sense along the way? When there are a lot of variables to look at, we should allow the computer with machine learning to go through it all and figure out what is there. But we still need to be the second eyes or ears that are on it to see what is there.

While the machine is able to get some amazing results in a short amount of time, we have to remember that it is not always invincible in this process, and we need to make sure that it is going to work well. We are able to take a look at it with some fresh eyes, and then figure out whether it all makes sense or not. We have to be that second pair of eyes though, or this process is going to end up failing us along the way.

What Can Machine Learning Do?

Now that we have a bit more information on machine learning and how amazing it can be for some of our own success, it is time for us to dive in to some of the different things that we are able to do when we bring out the technology and some of the algorithms that come with machine learning. There are actually a lot of different things that we are able to use machine learning for overall if we just take the time to learn what they are and how we are able to benefit from them overall. Some of the different ways that companies are using machine learning, and how you may be using machine learning too without realizing it would include the following:

Helping us to detect spam in our email. Think about how tedious and boring it would be if you had to spend all of your tie sorting through emails and seeing which ones were spam and which ones were important. This would take forever, and we would probably give up on using email overall in the first place. This is where machine learning is going to come into play. Most of the major email providers that we use today, such as Gmail, will use techniques of machine learning in order to filter out spam emails.

This works because the algorithm that will run the email server will be trained on data first. The data it is trained on will include past emails that were spam so that it knows which phrases and words and even which email addresses are likely to be spam. Over time, it will even be able to get better at the job, and this can provide you with some powerful coding in the process. Sometimes, spam gets through, but it is a whole lot less than what you would get if this information we're able to just get through.

The next way that machine learning is able to help us out is with face recognition. With this kind of task, machines are able to identify someone just from a photo, and sometimes, from videos as the technology continues to progress as well. For example, we can use this to figure out who is authorized to go into a certain system, to get onto email, or just to recognize who is in a picture on Facebook, for example.

One of the methods of machine learning that you are likely to use on a regular basis is speech recognition. If you have used some of the popular assistants that are able to recognize your voice and respond to you, such as Alexa or your own phone for that matter, then you have seen one of the more popular applications of machine learning already at work.

There are a lot of devices that we use today that are going to rely on speech recognition in order to get things done. This can include options like Google Now and Amazon Echo just to name a few. The fundamental idea of these is that there can be interactions between the computer and the human through voice. And the more times that you use the device, the more it can learn your own individual speech patterns and what you are requesting, and the better it is at helping get things done.

The next option that we are able to see when it comes to how well machine learning can help us get things done is with the help of computer vision and image classification. We can see this when we take a look at Google Photos. This is a technology that is able to create some image filtering based on an object or a person we decide on.

Facebook is working with this as well. Their AI research lab is always looking for some new ways in order to improve the experiences of the user through things like image classification. The hope with this is to make it so that even those who are blind can have the AI describe the content that is in an image.

Many marketers are working with machine learning as well. This helps them to reach the right customers at the right times when they place their ads and makes it so that they are not wasting money along the way either. Some of the different advertisements that we are already seeing would be options like sponsored ads or Google Ad Sense. We may also see this with some of the recommendation engines out there like Amazon and Netflix.

The anti-virus that you rely on can work with this idea as well. Many viruses are going to change over time, and knowing what is going to happen next is hard. These programs are able to learn from the viruses and attacks in the past and use that information in order to block new attacks, even if these attacks are ones that the program did not notice in the past or has never encountered.

Healthcare is a bit option that is going to use machine learning in many cases. For example, it can be used to help us to detect the diseases that someone is going through in some of the earlier stages of the process. It can make a diagnosis of problems just as efficiently as a human but often faster and can help our medical professionals get better at the work that they are doing on a regular basis. It can even come in and help as virtual assistants to make things so much easier overall as well.

These are just a few of the options where we are going to see that machine learning, and some of the features that come with it are going to be useful for businesses throughout all sorts of industries. Many companies are excited to start looking at machine learning and all that it is able to do because there is just so much potential that comes with this kind of programming. When we are able to put it all together, we will find that these are going to be some of the best things that you can do for your business as a whole.

As it stands right now, many experts agree that what we are currently able to do with machine learning is just the tip of the iceberg. It is likely that as more time goes on, we are going to be able to find more and more situations where we would use this kind of technology, and this can really change the way that the world of business works.

Into the Future
Every company that is taking a look at machine learning is going to have its own wishlist for what they would like this to do for them. Wishful thinking, when it is put into action, is eventually

something that can come true. In the near future, it is possible to work with machine learning in ways that we never thought possible in the past, and there are often many solutions and uses for this that we would never imagine in the first place. That is just the power of machine learning on its own.

For example, in the future, Adobe would like to be able to add in some more integration between what we are able to do with machine learning and the customer experience. They would like to be able to integrate data streams from social media, apps, websites, and more. This could help them to reach their customers better and really be able to take a more holistic approach when it comes to their marketing campaigns as well.

There is just so much that this kind of technology is going to be able to do for us in the future, and it is important that we learn all of the different ways that we are able to use it for some of our own needs as well. Any business, no matter what industry they are in, will be able to benefit when we work with machine learning and all of the neat things that it is able to do, and we definitely need to spend some of our time learning more about this method and how we are able to use it for some of our own needs as well, whether this helps us to reach your customers, to find new ways of doing business, reducing waste, and so much more.

Chapter 4: The K-Nearest Neighbor Algorithm

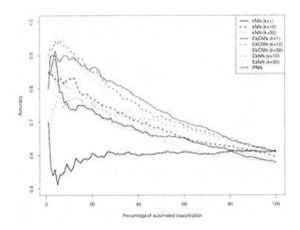

Now that we have had some time to take a look at the machine learning that we will want to work with, and we know more about some of the benefits and more that we are able to do with that machine learning, it is time for us to dive in and learn more about some of the different algorithms that we are able to handle with this kind of process. There are so many different algorithms that are going to fit under the term of machine learning, and the number is growing all of the time as more and more programmers try to jump on board and use this, or find that the available algorithms are not really what they need for that particular project they are focusing on.

The first out of the algorithms that we are going to spend some of our time on will be known as the KNN or the K-Nearest Neighbors algorithm. This is a non-linear classification model, and it is going to be considered one of the supervised machine learning algorithms that we talked about before. This means that the data we have to provide to this algorithm needs to be labeled for us ahead of time or it is not going to work.

When it comes to working with the KNN algorithm, you will find that there are a lot of benefits, and it is going to be able to help you handle a lot of the different projects that you would like. When we are working on this KNN algorithm, you may find that it is really useful when we would like to be able to cut down on some of the noise that is going to sometimes show up in the set of data that you are trying to work with.

Depending on what kind of data you are working with at the time, or how much of it you gathered from a lot of different places over time, and from which sources, you may find that some of the outliers and noise that comes with your data is going to be loud. When we are able to cut down on some of this noise, we will find that it is easier to see the real information that we need inside and will ensure that the results that we are able to get out of any algorithm that we choose to use, but especially the KNN algorithm, is going to be as accurate as possible.

There are many algorithms that we are able to work with when it comes to working with machine learning. This makes it hard to know why you would want to work with this kind of algorithm over some of the others. The benefits of working with the KNN algorithm and why you would want to choose it over some of the other options include:

1. It can work well with problems, even if they are considered multi-class.
2. You are able to apply this algorithm to both problems that are regressive and those that are classification.
3. There aren't any assumptions that come up with the data. This ensures that you get the information that you want, rather than having any assumptions in the place causing some issues.
4. It is an easy algorithm to work with. It is easy to understand, especially if you are brand new to the machine learning process.

However, we will find that there are going to be some more options for some of the algorithms that you are able to choose from because this algorithm, though it has a lot of benefits that go along with it, is not going to work in each situation that you want to use when it comes to machine learning. Along with some of the benefits that we talked about earlier, there are a few negatives of this algorithm and a few situations where you are likely to not want to use this for your needs. Some of the negatives of this algorithm, and why you need to do your research rather than just jumping in and working with this option, include the following:

1. It is going to be computationally and memory-intensive expensive. If you don't have the right system and the right amount of space to work with, it is going to make it more difficult to see the results that you want from this algorithm.
2. If there are a lot of independent variables that you are going to work with, you will find that the KNN algorithm is going to struggle.
3. The KNN algorithm isn't going to work that well if you have any rare event or skewed, target variables.
4. Sensitive to the scale of data.

For any of the problems that we are going to work with, you will find that having a smaller value of k is going to give us more variance in any of the predictions that we are working with. In addition, when you set it so that k is at a bigger value, it is possible that there is going to be more bias in the model as you work on it too.

While you are working with this one though, there may be times when you will need to go through and create some dummy variables. This is going to make it easier to figure out the categorical variables that will show up in this algorithm. This is different than the regressions that we will look for though because you can work with creating the k dummies rather than just the k-1.

With some of this in mind when we start, we then need to make sure that we are finding some of the best methods that will help us to find these values for k in the first place before we get too far. There are a few methods that a programmer is able to use to make this happen, but often, the best option to ensure that the information is accurate and will do what you would like is to work with cross-validation.

Cross-validation is a great process to use, but it is most important because we are able to use this to help us figure out a good estimation of what the error of validation is going to be right from the start, ensuring that we know what to expect and helping us to make some smart decisions when it comes to whether we want to use this algorithm on our data or not. To make sure that this is going to happen in the manner that we want though, we have to make sure that one of the subsets of our training set it withheld from the process when we build up the model so that we can use it for this purpose later on.

Cross-validation is going to be the process where we are able to go through and then divide up the training data in a manner that is as random as possible. For the example that we are going to spend some time talking about here, we are going to work with a validation that is meant to be 10-fold. This means that we are going to take all of the data that we are using for training and then divide it into ten groups.

When we are doing the dividing up, we want to make sure that we are keeping these as close to the same size as we can. From this, about 90 percent of the data that we are using in each set is going to be used to train the model we have. Then the other ten percent, or as close to that as possible when we get started, is going to be used to validate that the model is working and will help us to do some testing before we rely on that model for our business decisions along the way. If we find that the cross-validation is not giving us results that are any good in the process, then this is a sign that we need better data, we need more data for training or that something is wrong with the algorithm.

Another thing that we need to focus on here is the misclassification rate. The one that is the most important to what we are doing in this part is the ten percent that we actually took out of the data for training and held to work on the validation. This procedure is going to be something that we need to go through more than once and repeat to make sure that we are validating all of the work that we are doing here.

Since we are focusing our attention on doing a 10-fold validation, that means that we are planning to go through the cycle ten times. We will train the data with some information in the first set, and then cross-validate it with the data that is held behind in the first place. Then we do the same with the second set, the third set, the fourth set, and all the way through until all of your data is handled. Each of the groups of observations that we decide to work with here and run will be seen as the validation, and then it is also possible to test through this as well to help you get the best results.

As we can see, working with the KNN algorithm is not as difficult as it may seem in the beginning. But it is going to provide us with some awesome ways to learn more about our data and what is inside. And if you go through the process of training and then working with cross-validation along the way, in a manner similar to what we were discussing above, you will find that it is going to provide us with some accurate results in the end, even if it does seem to take a bit longer to go through the training set.

Chapter 5: Creating a Neural Networks

Another option that we are going to spend some time on when it comes to handling our data and making sure that it works out the way that we want is to work with some neural networks. This is another thing that works well with the Scikit-Learn library and will help us to really get the results that we want. These are going to be really strong to work with and can be a neat thing for machine learning because of all the power that comes with them.

To start with, these neural networks are going to work in a similar manner to what we see in the human brain. This will be able to help us to look through data, pick up on some of the different patterns that are there, and more. And when it makes the right predictions, it is able to form some stronger connections and will remember that information in the future as well. And it can even learn from the mistakes and the times when the neural network is not working the way that we would like, then it will be able to learn from that and really make some changes to learn better next time.

Any time that we decide to work with one of these neural networks, we are going to find that there are going to be quite a few layers that will show up with these. And all of these layers are going to take some time to look to see whether there are patterns on this or not. If the network finds that there is a layer where it is able to find a pattern, it will hold onto that before going on to the following layer.

This process is going to continue on through the layers until the neural network is not able to find any more patterns for the process. When it has been able to get to this point, the neural network finds that it is at the end of the job and will use the patterns and more that it has been able to find and will then make a prediction based on that information.

There are going to be a few things that we will be able to find happening at this point in the process. The results that you will get depend on how this program is able to work. If the algorithm that you set up with the neural network went through this process and followed the steps that were above, and then properly sorted through all of the layers, then it will be able to make a good prediction in the process.

If the neural network is accurate with its prediction, then the neurons of the system are going to remember this and will strengthen, ensuring that the neural network will be more accurate the next time it goes through. This is because the program has been able to work with artificial intelligence and machine learning in order to form the strong associations between the object and the patterns. The more times that this system provides us with the right answers, the more efficient it will be when it is time to turn it on and work with it again.

Now, this may seem a little bit far fetched and like it isn't something that could actually happen. But a closer examination of these neural networks will help us to see how they work together and why they are so important. For our example, let's say that your goal is to create a program that is able to take a picture that you input into it, and then, by looking at that picture and going through the layers, the program is able to recognize that the image in that picture is that of a car.

If the program has been set up in the proper manner, it is going to make the right prediction that there is a car in the picture. The program is able to come up with this prediction based on some of the features that it already knows belongs to the car, including the color, the number on the license plate, the placement of the doors, the headlights, and more.

With this one, we need to make sure to remember there is the potential for many layers to show up, but the good news is that the more layers we are able to go through with our images, the more accurate the predictions are going to be overall. If your neural network can make some accurate predictions, then it is going to be able to learn this lesson and will hold onto it along the way and will get faster and more efficient at making the predictions later on.

The next thing that we need to look at when it comes to neural networks is that they are able to remember some of the work that they were able to accomplish in the past. So, if you present the neural network with a picture of a car, and then the neural network is accurate at making a prediction that the image that shows up in the picture was a car, it is able to remember its predictions later similar to what we would see with a human who is learning as well.

Then, later on, if you give the neural algorithm a picture of a car, especially if the second image is similar to the first one that you showed to the algorithm earlier on, it is going to remember the lesson it did before and will use that to make a quick and efficient prediction again. The algorithm will be able to get through the different layers that come with this image quickly and will provide us with a prediction of a car, and it will be able to do this in a lot less time than before. Just think about all of the ways that we would potentially be able to work with this kind of technology, and this algorithm, to make sure that we can learn from the information that we have available already.

Chapter 6: The Linear Classifier Algorithm

As we are working through some of the problems that we want to handle in machine learning, there may be some situations in supervised learning where two of the biggest tasks that you need to spend your time on will need to have some linear classification and linear regression. The linear regression is sometimes going to come into play because it is going to help us to predict some of the value that we have in our data. But then we are also able to work with the linear classifier because it is going to put more attention into some of the classes that are so important with the Python language.

No matter which of these methods you like to use with machine learning, you will be able to do some powerful things with your own coding. In this chapter though, we are going to spend a bit of our time looking at the linear classifier and look at the different steps that you are able to see when it is time to work with this type of machine learning.

To start with though, you will find that the most prevalent type of machine learning that you are able to work with is problems of classification. In fact, a good 80 percent of what you are going to do in machine learning will rely on these classification problems. The main goal that you are going to spend your time on when it comes to classification is to use these algorithms to make a good prediction on how likely it is that a class is actually going to happen, based on the inputs that you use with it, the label, and the class at hand.

If you have a dependent variable or a label and they only come in with two of the classes that you plan to work with from the very beginning, then you know that the algorithm that you are focusing on is going to be a binary classifier. If you would like to work with one of the classifiers but you would like to have it work with more than one class, this means that it is possible for it to tackle any of the labels that have three or more classes at a time. We can explore this a bit later on.

We can take a look at one of the examples of this ahead of time though. Many of the classification problems that we have that we would also say are binary would be able to make a prediction for us about how likely one of our customers will come back and make a second or third purchase after that one. But if you want to take a different angle and would like to see the system make a prediction about the animal type that you place into an image, you will need to work with more of a multiclass kind of classification. This is because it is possible that more than two animal types can show up in the picture that you are working with.

Now we need to take a look at some of the steps that we are able to take in order to measure out our linear classifier performance. Accuracy is always going to be important when we are working in machine learning because it will ensure that we are actually getting the results that we need when we rely on them. The performance of this kind of classifier overall is going to be measured with the accuracy metric, and that should show us just how important this metric is going to be.

When we take a look at the accuracy though, it is going to be a good measurement of whether or not our algorithm is able to take in the right values and then divide that number by how many observations are actually present in your work. The higher the accuracy that we are able to get here, the better it is for some of our work and what we can rely on out of this algorithm.

We can take a look at how this is going to work. For example, if you are setting up the value of accuracy to be a minimum of 85 percent, this means that the algorithm will need to be right 85 percent of the time. On the other hand, this same algorithm is going to end up being wrong about 15 percent of the time. If you are working with numbers and plan to use the data you have to make some good predictions, then it is important that your accuracy ends up being as high as possible.

As we look more at the accuracy, we need to keep in mind that there can be some shortcomings with this kind of metric. This is always going to show up when you take a look at the class of imbalance. A data set that is not balanced all that well is going to occur when the observations that you have in the algorithm isn't able to equal all of the groups that you are using in this as well.

To help us get a better understanding of how this is going to work, we can say that we are focusing our attention on the challenge of classifying a rare event using some logistics. In this case, we would need to take some time to think about the classifier that is the best to work with, and that would include something like estimating how many patients passed on maybe when they were in contact with a specific disease. In the data that you are presented with, you may find that the set tells you that about five percent of the patients who contracted this disease died from it.

With this information in mind, you would then be able to bring in the linear classifier algorithm and train it so that it was able to predict how many deaths are likely to happen from the general population if they get the disease, and even make predictions on who is the most likely to die if they caught the disease. This metric of accuracy is then going to be in order to help us evaluate the performance of a hospital or clinic. If the average of deaths of patients who die from this disease is 5 percent, and a hospital is at two percent, then their performance is doing well. But if the average of a hospital is at 10 percent, then there may need to be some changes to prevent as many deaths from this disease.

The other thing that we need to focus on next is going to be something that we can call the confusion matrix. This is going to be one of the better ways that we are able to look at how a classifier is able to perform compared to some of the accuracies that we had above. This matrix is going to help us to see how our classifier will perform when we can compare it to the accuracy that we had above. When you decide to bring in our confusion matrix, you will start to get a good visual about the classifier and its accuracy by comparing the predicted, and the actual, classes to one another.

Keep in mind with this one that the confusion matrix that turns out to be binary is going to consist of squares. If you decide that this is the matrix that you would like to work with, there are a few parts that can come with it including the following:

1. TP: This is going to be known as the true positive. This is going to contain all of the predicted values that were correctly predicted as an actual positive.

2. FP: This is going to be the false ones or the ones that were predicted in an incorrect manner. They were usually predicted as positive, but they were actually negative. This means that the negative values show up, but they had been predicted ahead of time as positive.

3. FN: This is a false negative. This is when your positive values were predicted as negative.

4. TN: This is going to be the true negative. These are the values that were predicted in a correct manner and were predicted as actual negative.

When you have a programmer who is able to take a look at this kind of matrix and can use it in the proper manner, they are going to end up with a ton of information to work with. The confusion matrix is going to help us to really look at the predicted class, and compare it over to the actual class that we get, to help us compare and contrast what is going on with that data as well.

The final thing that we need to take a look at here is whether or not the precision and the sensitivity is going to be important with some of the work that we will do. The confusion matrix is going to end up being one of the best things that we can focus on when it is time to look at our linear classifications and when we want to gain a better understanding of the information that our data is holding onto.

But when we do decide to work with this kind of matrix, you will find that it opens up the door to a ton of information showing up along the way. These matrices are worth the time though because they will provide you with a lot of information, especially when we are looking at the false and true positives inside of some of the information that we have. However, even though this is a great thing for us to work with, there will be some cases when it is better to work on a metric that is more concise so that we can better understand whatever information we are going through.

To help us get through this a bit more, we need to take a closer look at the metric that we would like to use. And the first metric is precision. This is an important metric to spend our time on because it will really show us how accurate our class will be. This may not make a lot of sense, but it basically means that the precision metric is really going to help us to get a measure of how likely the positive class prediction is going to turn out correct in the long run. The formula that we are able to run to show this will include:

Precision = TP / (TP + FP)

The maximum score that we are going to have when we do this will show up here. And this is going to show us the classifier and be right when we have a positive value in place. While precision and a good look at how precise one of our metrics is before we start are important to our success, it is not going to be the only metric that we want to spend our time on at all. We also want to spend some time taking a look at how sensitive the metric is as well.

This sensitivity is going to be important because it is going to let us know how much the ratio of the positive classes in the algorithm is and how often they can make the accurate predictions that you are looking for. This is a good metric to work with because it is going to help us to take a look at the positive formula that is there and can make sure that we will be able to check whether things are lining up in the manner that we want. If you would like to check what the sensitivity of your algorithm is ahead of time, then you will need to work with the following formula to help:

Recall = TP / (TP + FN)

Chapter 7: Working with Recurrent Neural Networks

When we were doing some work earlier on in this guidebook, remember that we did bring up the topic of neural networks and all of the neat things that they will be able to do for us to get the work done. Remember that these neural networks are going to be on a kind of learning curve. What this means is that when they are able to provide us with the right answer, the connections that are there will grow stronger, which allows them to make better predictions based on the information that they in the past, to make stronger predictions.

What this means for us is that these neural networks are able to work in a manner that is similar to how the human learns and remembers things. This can make it a stronger and much more efficient method to work with overall, especially when it comes to how it is able to handle some of the decisions that it makes later on. And when it has some time to learn and do more work, the neural network is going to get so much better at making some of the good predictions that we need.

Now that we have some of that information down, it is time for us to go back a bit and look more at these neural networks, and get a better understanding of how they are going to work in mimicking the learning that the human brain is able to do. The first thing that we are able to handle here is how the brain is going to work. You may notice from your own experience that the brain is not going to be in the habit of restarting its thinking patterns every few seconds. If this were true, then it would be impossible for any of us to accomplish anything or learn anything very well.

The brain is able to work, and we are able to progress and learn because we have the ability to build up anything that we were able to learn about in the past. This past could be as recent as a few minutes ago, or it could be some of the things that we were able to learn as a child. As we go through some of the different parts that we learned about in this guidebook, it is likely that you understand the patterns and the words and some of the ideas, based on what we explored earlier on. This is how we are able to really put it all together and see some amazing progress in the process.

This is going to be important because it is going to show us that the thoughts and some of the different parts of learning that we gain are going to stick with us when we work with persistence and consistency. This is going to be the idea that we are able to use when it is time to work on the recurrent neural network. In most situations, the neural network that we explored in an earlier chapter will not be able to get all of this done for us, and honestly, that is often one of the reasons that people may not like to use it, especially with some of the paths that machine learning is going to do in the future.

There are a few methods that we can use to help us think about it. First, if you would like to be able to take some events and then classify them based on what happens inside of a movie, for example, it is going to be hard to get a traditional form of the neural network to reason through this option. The reason with this one is that the neural network is not going to be able to remember all of the parts that show up in the code in this manner.

The neat thing that we are going to see with this one though is that we are able to bring in the recurrent neural network to help us address this big problem when we are working in machine learning. The recurrent neural network is going to be pretty similar to what we see with the traditional neural network, but it is going to focus more on being a loop, which allows the information to stick around after the network has been able to learn about it.

With this kind of neural network, the loop that you see is going to allow any of the information that is on the network to be learned and then will pass from one part of the network over to another one as needed. This is going to be an idea that is pretty similar to having more than one copy of your network, and then each of the messages that you need will move down the line in a pattern as well.

The chain nature that we are going to see here is able to help us to reveal that these kinds of the network will be related back to a list and a sequence in many situations. They are also going to be an architecture type that is pretty natural for neural networks so that they are able to use the data that they want. And we have to work with these on a regular basis to keep them sharp and working in the manner that we would like.

Over the past few years, there has been a lot of success when we are able to take the methods of these networks and adding them to machine learning. And in the process, we are able to use this kind of method in order to help us handle a lot of different types of machine learning like automatic translation, image captioning, modeling of languages, and speech recognition.

As we take a look back at some of the neural networks that we spent our time on earlier, we are going to see that there is a big limitation when it comes to having a lot of constraints that are on the API that we use. These constraints are likely going to only take a vector that provides them with an input that is known ahead of time, and then they are going to only be able to produce a vector that is fixed in size when we use the output. Keep in mind that this is just the beginning of the issues and problems that we are going to be able to work with when we choose the recurrent neural network for some of our needs.

To make it a little bit easier for us to see how the recurrent neural network is going to work for our needs, and why they are going to be better for us to work with when it comes to these networks compared to the traditional methods, we will need to take a look at the chart that we have above to make sure we can handle all of this. When we look at that chart, we are going to see that each part is going to have a few rectangles that we need to focus on, and we can look at each of these parts as one of the vectors that we will focus on. And then the arrows that we see in between all of these can help us to see what will happen in the functions and which direction they are supposed to take.

When it is time for us to input the vectors, we are going to be able to distinguish these vectors away from the other options because they are going to show up in red. Then the output vectors are going to be brought up inside of this and will be in blue this time. Then there is a third color in this graph, which is the green vectors and those will hold onto the state of the RNN.

Taking a closer look at the chart that is above, and helping us to read it from left to right, we are able to see how all of the parts are going to work in our recurrent neural network, and why all of these are so important to some of the things that we want to work wit:

1. The first part that we will want to work with is the processing mode that is vanilla. This one means that we not going to focus on the RNN at all. This is going to mean that the input we are working with will end up being fixed, along with the output. We can call this one the image classification as well.

2. Then we are able to work with the sequence output. This second part is going to be the image captioning that we are going to be taken with an image, and then, when it has had some time to look at the image, it is going to provide us with some words to describe what is going on.

3. The sequence input is going to be the third part that we need to focus on. This is going to fall into the third picture that we have above and it is seen more like the analysis that is sentimental because it is going to show us the sentence that is given, and then will help us to figure out whether the sentiment that is used with it is positive or negative in the process.

4. We then need to take a look at the sequence output and input. You will find that this one is going to be shown off in the fourth box. It is going to be similar to what we find with machine translation and it is when the RNN that we have is able to read out a sentence in the English

language. Then it is able to take some of the information and will give us an output that is able to read out the sentence in another language like French.

5. And then we are able to take a look at the last and final box that is present in all of this. This one is going to be the synced sequence input and output that we are able to work with. A good example of this one is going to be the video classification and it is a good one to help us when we want to label out all of the frames that are going to occur in a video if we decide that we would like to work with it in this manner.

When we have had some time to go through and check all of this out, we can then double-check whether the constraints that we need are in place or if they are missing. If you did this well, you will see that some of the constraints that will talk about the lengths of the sequences we would like to list out ahead of time are not going to be there. The reason that we see this is that the recurrent transformation, or the part that we will see with the green rectangles, will be fixed during this process. This is a good thing because it allows us to apply it as often as we would like in order to get things to work.

It is now time to take some of this information and look at how we are able to work with it in the RNN or focus on the green parts of our chart above. This is where we need to make sure that the RNN is trained in the right mode. Basically, we are using the character-level language model, which means that we are going to be able to supply this with a lot of text and data, and then, once it has had a chance to look at and hopefully learn from the data, we are going to request that it does something for us.

This is also the step where we would want the neural network to model the probability of the distribution of the character that is going to show up next when we have a sequence going on. And this can happen with the RNN if we base it on the sequence that we provided into it during training. This is going to help us to show up with some new text, or it can help us when it is time to do decoding, even if you do plan to just work with one of these characters at a time.

We can take a look at a good example of how this is going to work for our needs. Let's say that we are starting out with vocabulary in a new language that is limited, and we only have four letters that are possible to work with, the four letters of the helo. With this kind of information, we want to make sure that the RNN can be trained to do a training sequence so that it is able to list out "hello" instead of the other option. This sequence is going to be a source of four different training models that we are able to put together to ensure that we are going to get things to work the way that we want, even if we are only able to input or receive one character out of this at a time.

This is going to seem complex to work with, but you will find that when we go through it one step at a time, and see how this is supposed to work, we will be able to get all of it to work, and you will soon recognize how this is going to help us out in the long run. Some of the different parts that we need to look at here and consider along the way to get things done are the following:

1. The probability of getting "e" should be just as likely to occur as getting the letter "h".
2. "L should be likely in the context of "he"
3. The "l" should also be likely if the system is given the context of "hel"

4. "o" should be likely if the other sequences have happened and the context of "hell" is in place.

This means that we are going to be ready to encode all of the characters that show up in our vector, and we need to work with the l of k in coding. This is done because it is going to help us to get all zeroes except for a single one at the index of the character in the vocabulary. With this information, we need to find a way to feed them in so the RNN can read them, doing the characters one at a time, and then we can use the right functions to help out with this.

Once we have been able to go through the steps above and gotten the text to show up in the order that we would like, we need to spend some time doing the observations that are needed on the sequence of the output vectors in 4-D. One of these dimensions is going to be with each of the characters that we are hoping to show up in all of this. We are then able to interpret this in a manner based on the confidence that we want to place in this system, and how well we think the neural network is going to be able to come in and assign the characters at the right time and int eh right order.

The diagram that we are able to see below is going to show us a better idea of how this kind of distribution is supposed to work for us:

Out of this, we may use an example of seeing that in the first time step, the RNN would see the character of "h" it was able to assign some confidence to this of 1.0, to the next letter turning into "h", 2.2 to getting the letter "e" -3.0 to "l" "and 4.1 to "o". Since the training data that we are using, (which is the string of hello that we talked about above), had the next right character being "e" we want to increase the confidence or the green color, and then decrease how confident it is in all of the other letters, which are going to be shown in the red above.

In addition to some of the information that we are going to see here, there is going to be an additional step that we are able to go through that will help us to get to the desired character target out of the four that we are able to work with here as well. And we want to make sure that we have a lot of confidence before we ever use it that the network is able to handle this kind of work.

This step is going to be a bit harder to handle compared to some of the others, but it is something that we need to focus some of our attention on because the more confidence that we are able to add into this, the easier it is to see that the system or the algorithm will be able to get the results that we want as the output.

So, since we are working on the process of making sure the RNN behaves properly, and this means that it is going to have some operations that are differentiable along the way, we first need to bring in one of the algorithms that we are using here for the process of backpropagation.

This is something that may sound a bit confusing and hard to work in the first place, but basically, it is going to be known as the recursive application of the chain rule that you may have heard about before when you did calculus. The reason that we are going to focus on this is that it helps us to find the right direction to take for adjusting all of the weights in the information. This helps us to increase the scores in the targets that we want while leaving everything else the same.

Then we are able to go through and work on updating the parameters. This is going to be something that we need to work with because it takes all of our weights along the way and will nudge them up a bit so that they go in the direction that we need to make this work. If it is possible, it is best to double-check all of the inputs that we are using to help ensure that we can feed them into the RNN and still get everything to end up even when we are all done. And then when the parameter is able to finish the update, you should find that the score of all the characters will fit inline the way so that you get the right answers.

Now, keep in mind that when you run this the first time, it may not be as accurate as you would like. This means that we will need to go through this process a few times to help make sure that all of the accuracy and precision that we want to work with will be there. This is a frustrating thing in some cases because it is not going to be as clear-cut as we might like as a beginner and there will not be a set number of times when we will need to do this. You have to consider the data points that you are working with, and how complex the situation is as well, and then go from there until the accuracy is right.

So, let's say that we start out with something simple like the "hello" code that we had earlier in this chapter. With a code that is this simple, it is not going to take too long to get the RNN to work and get the confidence that is needed ahead of time. But if you are taking these same ideas and trying to have it decade a large book or a ton of words, then this one, of course, is going to take more tries and more energy in order to accomplish.

As we start to work with these neural networks more and more, you are going to eventually get to the time of testing. This is important because it is going to provide us with some of the certainty that we need to know that we are feeding in the characters necessary to this algorithm. And once we have been able to feed these characters into the system, then it is time to make sure that the distribution you are working with will describe which characters your system is able to bring out next. As you work on this program we should take a few moments to look it over to see whether it is doing this well and providing you the right information before you proceed and waste more time when things are not going well.

Now, if you are doing the steps above and find that your algorithm is not providing you with the answers that you would like the first time around, which is possible, this just means that you need to work on it a bit and train it some more ahead of time to get it to work. It does not mean that the RNN failed and that you should never work with it again. This is an algorithm that is able to learn as it goes, so if you find that it is not providing you with the answers that you would like, then you just need to go through the process a few more times to get it all set up and ready to go. You will need to do this as many times as it takes in order to make sure that the neural network is going to behave in the way that you would like.

We spent quite a bit of time in this chapter taking a look at these recurrent neural networks and all of the things that they are able to do to help us get the work done and see some of the results that we would like as well. But some of the coding that we are able to do with them, and the way that they can help us to work on our networks and see some results from our data, is amazing and it is so important to learn how to make these work for some of our needs.

The RNN algorithm is going to be really powerful and it is able to provide us with a lot of the answers that we need to our common machine learning questions, often at a better rate than we are able to use with the other algorithms that are out there. When you are ready to work with this kind of algorithm for some of your own needs, make sure to go through some of the steps that we have above and see how this is going to be able to benefit you as well.

Chapter 8: Clustering Algorithms

While we are learning more about machine learning and some of the neat things that you are able to do with all of this, it is time for us to take a look at the algorithm known as the K-Means clustering. This is going to be one that shows up quite a bit and can help you to get more accomplished with the coding that you do. The basic idea that comes with this one is that you are able to take the data from the system, all of it that we have not been able to label yet, and then we are going to put it together into some clusters to see what is going on.

The main goal that we are going to see when we handle some of these clusters is that the objects that all into the same cluster with one another are going to be related to one another closely and they will not come in with as many similarities to the options that fall into the other clusters that you have. The similarity that you see with the items that are in the same clusters is going to be the metric that we are able to use to see how strong the relationship between the objects of data can be.

The field of data mining is then able to work with the algorithm of clustering quite a bit. This is going to be really true if you are going to do some kind of exploration. But this is not going to be the only kind of field that will see some benefit from this algorithm. It is also possible to use it in some fields like information retrieval, data compression, pattern recognition, image analysis and so much more.

The K-Means clustering algorithm is also going to work and form some clusters that we would like, based on how similar the values that you have in the data are to one another. You can then go through and specify what you would like to see with the values of K, which will simply be how many clusters you are hoping to work with here and how many parts you want to try and split the data into. This depends on what you are hoping to get out of it. If you just want to sort through the males and females who shop at your store, you only need two clusters. If you want to sort out into more you can do that as well.

This clustering algorithm is going to start out by helping us figure out what value will be the center of all our clusters and then it is going to go through a total of three other steps to help make this happen including:

1. You will want to start with the Euclidian distance between each data instance and the centroids for all of the clusters.
2. Assign the instances of data to the cluster of centroid with the nearest distance possible.

3. Calculate the new centroid values, depending on the mean values of the coordinates of the data instances from the corresponding cluster.

Now to work with this kind of algorithm, the input that we really need to look for to make the k-means happen is going to be found in the matrix for X. We are then able to go through this and check on the organization that is present for any choices to ensure that the rows you create are different samples each time, while each of the columns that you want to work with are going to have different factors as you work with them. If you are able to do this, you will only have to work with two steps to get it all done.

For our first step, we have to really consider the centers that we want to have for all of our clusters. The more of these clusters that we want to work with, the longer that this will take. If you are looking through the data and you are not that sure where to put the centers, then you may want to start out with some points that are more random and then see what happens with it. If things are not matching up in the manner that you would like with the help of this method, then you can always go through and try out a different center later on.

Then we can move on to the second step, and that is where we need to focus on the main loop. After you have had some time to work with the chosen centers, then you are able to decide where the data points will fit and which clusters they should work with as well. you can look at all of the samples that you have in order to figure out where to place these.

From this point in the game, we will need to spend some time on our recalculations to move around the centers of those clusters again. This time it needs to be based on the original points that each one was assigned. To make all of this happen, you just need to grab the samples that you have and figure out what the mean is on these as well. As soon as you get an answer for this one, then you will have your k-means ready to go.

This is not the end though. It is likely that we will need to head through these steps a few times before the convergence that this algorithm is looking for actually happens. For the most part though, based on the data amount that you have and where you are starting out, this can be done in five steps, and sometimes less. But if you are working on a complex problem with a lot of parts and there are many points of data that have a big variance, then it is possible that more steps are going to need to happen.

With this in mind though, we need to take a look at some of the coding that we are able to do in order to make this work for some of our needs as well. To start with here, we are going to look at how we are able to add in the k-means to the process.

But this is going to bring up the question of how we are supposed to make all of this happen so that we can find the k-means and create the clusters that we would like along the way.

One thing to keep in mind while we go through this is that the Euclidean distance is going to be important, and then we also need to focus on the cost of the functions put together to give us the results that we want. To make this easier, we need to take a look at some of the coding that will take over for this one. The best code to work with here to make all of this work will include:

```
import numpy as np
import matplotlib.pyplot as plt

def d(u, v):
  diff = u - v
  return diff.dot(diff)

def cost(X, R, M):
  cost = 0
  for k in xrange(len(M)):
  for n in xrange(len(X)):
  cost += R[n,k]*d(M[k], X[n])
  return cost
```

Take a moment to type this into your compiler to see how it is going to work for your needs as well. Once this is in the compiler and you have been able to go through and define the function in a manner so that the algorithm is going to plot out the results you are set to go. The plots will show up on the graph that you have, and it is going to basically turn into a scatterplot of information. There will be a few colors that are there because this will help us to notice the differences in the dots that we have and can make it easier to figure out the membership of the information that is found in each one. The coding to make this happen is easier than it may seem, and is going to include the following:

```
def plot_k_means(X, K, max_iter=20, beta=1.0):
N, D = X.shape
M = np.zeros((K, D))
R = np.ones((N, K)) / K

# initialize M to random
for k in xrange(K):
M[k] = X[np.random.choice(N)]

grid_width = 5
grid_height = max_iter / grid_width
random_colors = np.random.random((K, 3))
plt.figure()
```

```
costs = np.zeros(max_iter)
for i in xrange(max_iter):
# moved the plot inside the for loop
colors = R.dot(random_colors)
plt.subplot(grid_width, grid_height, i+1)
plt.scatter(X[:,0], X[:,1], c=colors)

# step 1: determine assignments / resposibilities
# is this inefficient?
for k in xrange(K):
for n in xrange(N):
R[n,k] = np.exp(-beta*d(M[k], X[n])) / np.sum( np.exp(-
beta*d(M[j], X[n])) for j in xrange(K) )

# step 2: recalculate means
for k in xrange(K):
M[k] = R[:,k].dot(X) / R[:,k].sum()

costs[i] = cost(X, R, M)
if i > 0:
if np.abs(costs[i] - costs[i-1]) < 10e-5:
break

plt.show()
```

Notice that when we are working with this kind of code above, the M and the R are going to stand out with their own matrices. To start, we can look at the R. This one is going to be found in a brand new matrix because it is going to hold onto the two indices that you need, namely the k and the n.

This doesn't mean that we can ignore what is going to happen with the M though. This one is going to be a matrix on its own as well. this is because it is going to include what is known as the D-dimensional vectors that come with K. The variable that will be considered the variable here is going to be responsible for helping us control how fuzzy, close together, or spread out the memberships of the clusters are. These will also be known as the hyperparameters that we discuss in other parts of this guidebook.

From all of this information, we will be able to go through and create a new main function that is able to create some of the rando clusters that we have, and then can call up the functions that we were able to define above. We are able to use a bit of Python coding to help us get this done, and this will include the following:

```
def main():
 # assume 3 means
 D = 2 # so we can visualize it more easily
```

```
s = 4 # separation so we can control how far apart the means
are
mu1 = np.array([0, 0])
mu2 = np.array([s, s])
mu3 = np.array([0, s])

N = 900 # number of samples
X = np.zeros((N, D))
X[:300, :] = np.random.randn(300, D) + mu1
X[300:600, :] = np.random.randn(300, D) + mu2
X[600:, :] = np.random.randn(300, D) + mu3

# what does it look like without clustering?
plt.scatter(X[:,0], X[:,1])
plt.show()

K = 3 # luckily, we already know this
plot_k_means(X, K)

# K = 5 # what happens if we choose a "bad" K?
# plot_k_means(X, K, max_iter=30)

# K = 5 # what happens if we change beta?
# plot_k_means(X, K, max_iter=30, beta=0.3)
```

```
if __name__ == '__main__':
  main()
```

We can already see from all of this that the Python language can take a task that seems pretty complicated and will divide it up in a manner that makes life a bit easier to handle and use as well. With the codes that we have been able to work within this chapter, we are basically setting it up so that we have our own k-means algorithm, and you should now have a much better understanding of how all of this is going to work.

You can now add in some data, with the help of the compiler that you are working with and the codes above and see what is going to happen when you work through all of this process as well. try out a few of these along the way and see how they work, and what you are able to do to make them work for your needs, and see how great they will be when creating some of the clusters that you would like with your data as well.

Chapter 9: Decision Trees and Turning Them Into Random Forests

Another option that we are able to take a look at when it comes to working with machine learning and all of the neat things that we are able to do with this kind of learning is going to be the decision trees and random forests. These kinds of algorithms are going to go together pretty well, and learning how to make them work for some of our own needs as well is going to be one of the best ways to ensure that we are able to get them to provide us with the answers that we need along the way.

Often we are going to find that the random forest and the decision tree are going to be found in the same kinds of topics in machine learning and that both of these algorithms are going to be able to work well together. These are going to be some efficient data tools that are able to help us to take on two of the choices that we would like to work with, and sometimes even more than two choices, especially when our choices are quite a bit different, and then we will use this information to help us figure out which decision out of the two (or more), that is going to be the best for your business and what you would like to be able to do in the future.

When you are looking at the future of your business and what you would like to do overall, it is possible that you will be presented with more than one option at a time. And sometimes, even though those options may be very different from one another, you will see that they are all good options and something that you would consider doing. But since you are only able to pick one because of them being so different or because of limited resources, you need to pick out a method that will help you to choose.

This is where the decision tree is going to come into play here. It is able to take your choices and then make some predictions on the outcomes of each one. When you are able to glance at these and see what the most likely outcome of each decision is, you can take out some of the risks that you will find with some of your decisions, and can actually choose the one that is right for you.

Now, you will find that there are a few different ways that you are able to work with these decision trees. Many of those who are working with machine learning will use it if either of their variables is categorical and one is random. However, there are times when you will need to use these decision trees with some of the classification problems that you have. To ensure that you are picking out and creating your decision tree well, then you need to make sure that you take all of the sets of data that you have and then split them up to be in two or more sets, with some similar data in each one. You can then sort this out with the help of independent variables because it will help you to set it up the way that the decision tree needs.

Sometimes, these decision trees are not going to end up acting in the manner that we need and sometimes it is better to take this out a bit more and work with two or more decision trees together. This is when the decision tree is technically going to switch over to a different type of algorithm that we are able to work with, and this one is going to be known as a random forest. Basically, the random forest is just going to be a collection of decision trees that we want to focus on.

The random forest algorithm is going to be a popular option to work with because they will help you to take a closer look at a lot of decisions that you may need to make for your business, and then will help you to see all of the possible outcomes of each one. You are then able to take a look at these and decide which decision is the best one for you.

As you can imagine already, there are going to be a lot of different applications that you will find when it comes to these random forests. This is because the random forest is going to be perfect when it is time for you to really take a look at some important decisions that you want to make, and then will help you to see the outcomes and choose based on this information. And often these random forests are going to do a great job at providing us with a clear-cut picture of our predictions and insights compared to some of the other options. Some of the ways that we are able to take on these random forests and get them to work in the manner that we would like includes:

- When you are working on your own training sets, you will find that all of the objects that are inside a set will be generated randomly, and it can be replaced if your random tree things that this is necessary and better for your needs.
- If there are M input variable amounts, then m<M is going to be specified from the beginning, and it will be held as a constant. The reason that this is so important because it means that each tree that you have is randomly picked from their own variable using M.
- The goal of each of your random trees will be to find the split that is the best for the variable m.
- As the tree grows, all of these trees are going to keep getting as big as they possibly can. Remember that these random trees are not going to prune themselves.
- The forest that is created from a random tree can be great because it is much better at predicting certain outcomes. It is able to do this for you because it will take all prediction from each of the trees that you create and then

will be able to select the average for regression or the consensus that you get during classification.

Random forests are a good tool that a programmer is able to use when they would like to make sure that they add in some data science to the machine learning that you are doing, and there are going to be many benefits. But any time that you are looking for an easy way to look through some of the options that are available for your work, and you want help making some smart decisions, then the decision trees and random forests will be the best option for you to choose.

As we can see here, there are a lot of times when we are going to be able to benefit from working with the random forests, and even with a simple decision tree if you are focused on just a few decisions rather than many. These both are going to help you to see the most likely outcome of a situation and can make it easier for you to really make sure that you understand what is going on with your options and choices at the time.

If these are set up and working in the proper manner, you will find that it is an easier way to see what is likely to happen based on the decision that you make, and it can lead you to make decisions that are based on facts and figures and data, rather than ones based on emotions and uncertainty. And we can all agree that this is going to be much better for the success of your business overall.

Chapter 10: The Support Vector Machines

While we are on the topics of some of the different algorithms that you are able to use when you work with machine learning, and how all of these are able to help us learn more about our data and what we are able to do with all of that data, it is time to take a look at the support vector machines, or the SVM. These are going to be the algorithms that we are able to use when we would like to take the data set that we are working with, and then plot all of the data so that they are able to show up on a plot that is n-dimensional. N is going to be all of the features that you are going to show on the chart as well.

It is possible for the programmer to go through and take on the value of these features, and work in order to translate all of this over to the value that you would use for some of your own chosen coordinates. The job that you are going to be able to do when it is time to get through to this point is to really learn where the hyperplane will fall. Sometimes, there are more than one of these hyperplanes to work with, and you need to make sure that you find the right one. The reason for this is that it is really able to show you what a difference there will be when we look at the classes that show up.

As we just mentioned, it is possible that you will find more than one of these support vectors showing up on your graphs in some cases. The good news with this though, so that you don't get too worried about it, is that not all of the vectors that you find are going to be important and you can usually tell which ones are important and which ones are not, with just a glance. Often, many of the vectors that you will see will just point to the coordinates of the individual observations that you are able to see there.

From this point then, you are able to work with the SVM algorithm in order to turn into the frontier, the part that is able to separate all of the different vectors that you have into classes, and then you will find the line that will need to be your hyperplane. And at this point, there are going to be two main parts that we will need to focus our attention on the most in order to get the results that we want.

Now, up until we got to this point, some of the different steps that we were talking about and looking through may seem a bit confusing, and you may worry that you will not be able to use this algorithm because of it. That is why we are going to take a detour here a bit and learn how we are able to get this to help us sort out our data and ensure that we see the best results.

First, we have to make sure that when we work with the SVM, that we are going to be able to find the hyperplane that will make all of this work the way that we would like. After you get some experience with this one, you will find that it is easier to get that hyperplane. But for a beginner, this is hard and it is possible that there will be two or more hyperplanes that are trying to get your attention at the same time as well.

This fact, that we are going to work with more than one hyperplane that we have to sort through is sometimes a big challenge for the beginner. You want to make sure that you are choosing the right hyperplane for the work that you want to do, rather than picking out the wrong one and then making all of the data fit it when it is not right.

The good thing to remember here is that even if you do have a few options when it comes to hyperplanes, there are still going to be some easy steps that we are able to use to help us pick out the right one. The specific steps that you are able to use when trying to figure out the hyperplane for your SVM will include:

- We are going to start out with three hyperplanes that we will call 1, 2, and 3. Then we are going to spend time figuring out which hyperplane is right so that we can classify the star and the circle.

- The good news is there is a pretty simple rule that you can follow so that it becomes easier to identify which hyperplane is the right one. The hyperplane that you want to go with will be the one that segregates your classes the best.

- That one was easy to work with, but in the next one, our hyperplanes of 1, 2, and 3 are all going through the classes and they segregate them in a manner that is similar. For example, all of the lines or these hyperplanes are going to run parallel with each other. From here you may find that it is hard to pick which hyperplane is the right one.

- For the issue that is above, we will need to use what is known as the margin. This is basically the distance that occurs between the hyperplane and the nearest data point from either of the two classes. Then you will be able to get some numbers that can help you out. These numbers may be closer together, but they will point out which hyperplane is going to be the best.

You will find that these support vector machines are going to be good options to spend some time on overall. They will help us to really get some of the work done that we would like and ensures that we are really able to handle the insights and predictions in a manner that is accurate and easy to understand as well.

Chapter 11: How to Work with Validation and Optimization Techniques

Now that we have had some time to look at some of the amazing techniques and algorithms that are available with machine learning, it is time for us to really get into some of the work that we are able to do to ensure these algorithms are smart and will work in the manner that we would like. In this chapter, we are going to take some time to look through the validation of an algorithm to make sure that it behaves the way that we would like. And from there we will be able to focus on how to optimize the techniques that we are focusing on so that they provide us with the best insights and predictions possible, and so we are actually able to get some good information out of them as well.

This is a lot to take in right from the start so we are going to take some time to talk about the different validation and optimization techniques that are out there, and what we are able to do with them to help us see the best results.

Techniques for Cross-Validation

The first validation technique that we are going to spend some time looking at in this chapter is going to be the cross-validation. With this one, we are going to take the algorithms of machine learning and then take our set of data and ensure that it is divided up into three parts. We will have the first part of the data be for training our algorithm, the second part for validating the algorithm, and then the third and final part is going to be used to test the algorithm and ensure it is working well.

The first set of data that we need to take a look at here when we are exploring some of the things that we can do with machine learning is the training set. This training set is going to be the part that we use to take our algorithm and rain it to behave the way that we would like. We will usually want to put about 60 percent of the data that we have available to work on training the model to make sure that it is going to work the way that you would like.

Then we are going to work with the data set that handles the validation. Once we have been able to select out a model that can perform well with the training set, it is time to run the model with our validation set. This is going to be a small subset of the data, and it is usually going to range from 10 to 20 percent of the data that you have. this set is going to help us with these models because it is going to give us an evaluation, without bias, of the fitness of the model. If the error on the data set for validation increases, then it is possible that we are working with a model that overfits.

And finally, we have the test data set. This is going to be new data that has never been used in the training at all. This is going to be a bit smaller but it is going to contain about 5 to 20 percent of the set of data that we have. and it is meant to help us test out the model evaluation that we are working on to see whether it is accurate or not.

In some cases, there is going to only be a training and a test set, and the programmer is not going to work with any validation set. There are some issues with this one though. Due to the sample variability between the test set and the training, the model is going to provide us with a better prediction on the data that we train but will fail to generalize on the test data. This can make us deal with a low error rate during training, but a high rate of an error on the testing phase of this process.

When we are able to go through and split up the sets of data that we have into the training test, and the validation set that we need, it is time to work with just one of the subsets of the data. Then it is possible to train this with fewer observations of the model. This helps when some of the subsets are not going to perform well, and then when this happens, we will see that it provides us with an overestimated test error rate for the model that is trying to get the whole set of to fit on that model you created.

To help us to solve both of these issues, we are going to work through this with an approach that is known as cross-validation. This is going to be one of the statistical techniques that will help us to partition the data so that it goes into subsets, which will allow us a way to train the data on one of the subsets. Then the rest of the data is going to be used to help us evaluate how well the model was able to perform and whether or not it did the work in the manner that we would like.

Now, to make sure that we are able to handle some of this work a little bit easier, and to ensure that we can reduce the amount of variability that will show up in this kind of data, we may go through and perform a lot of rounds of this cross-validation. But we will need to make sure that we are doing with this a new subset of the same data each time. We are then able to combine the validation results that we get out of these rounds so that we are going to get a better estimated of the predictive performance that we will get out of this model.

When we are doing with this, the cross-validation that we are focusing on is going to be able to provide us back with an estimate of the performance of that model, telling us which one is going to be the most accurate, compared to just doing this training one time and making an assumption that it is going to work the way that we want.

This may seem like a lot of information to keep track of right now, and it is a lot to hold onto. But with some of this information in mind, there are going to be a few techniques that we are going to see when it is time to bring out cross-validation, and some of these include:

1. Leave one out cross-validation or LOOCV: IN this one, we are going to take our set of data and divide it into two pairs to work on. In the first part, we are going to have a single observation, which is going to be the test data. And then in the second one, we are going to have all of the other observations that come in our set of data, and these will form up our training data.

   a. There are a few advantages to working with this one. First, we are going to find that there is far less

106

bias because we are going to use all of the set of data for training compared to some of the validation set approach where we are only working with part of the data to help with training.

b. There isn't going to be any randomness in the training or the test data because we will perform this many times and it will still give us the same results.

c. There are some disadvantages that come with this one as well. For example, MSE is going to vary as the test data is going to work with just one single observation. This sometimes adds some variability to the work. If the data point that you work with ends up being an outlier, then you will find that the variability is going to be much higher.

d. The execution of this model is going to be more expensive than some other options because the model has to be fitted n times rather than just once or twice.

2. K Fold cross-validation: This is going to be a technique of cross-validation that is going to take the set of data and randomly divide it into k groups or folds that are similar in size. The first fold that you have is going to be used for testing, and then the model is going to be

trained on k-1 folds. The process is going to be repeated K amount of times, and each time that you do this will have a different group of the data that you will use for validation.

    a. There are a few advantages that come with this one. First, the computation time is going to be reduced as we go through the process 10 times, or less, depending on what value you give to k.

    b. This one is also going to have a reduced bias so you can rely on the information that you have more.

    c. Every point of data gets to be tested just once and is used in training the k-1 times.

    d. The variance of the resulting estimate is going to be reduced the number of times that k increases.

    e. There are some disadvantages of k fold or the 10-old cross-validation. The training algorithm, compared to some of the other options, is going to be computationally intensive because the algorithm has to start over again and rerun from scratch k times to be effective.

3. When we are done with this part, we are going to move on to the stratified cross-validation. This is going to be another technique that works well because it is going to help us to arrange out the data so that each fold will be the right representation of the data set, and will force the

process so that all of the folds are going to have the least m instance for each class. This approach is going to work well because it will make sure that the data is not going to be overrepresented, especially when the variable that we would like to focus on with our target is not balanced out well.

    a. A good example of this is when we handle a problem of binary classification when we would like to predict whether or not someone who was on the Titanic was a survivor or not. We will then ensure that each of the folds that we have will include a percentage of the passengers who survived and a certain percentage of those who did not make it.

4. Another option that we are able to work with is known as the time-series cross-validation. This is where we see that splitting up our time series into a manner that is more random is not going to help us out as much. This is due to the fact that the time-related data is going to end up being messy. If we are working on figuring out the prices of the stocks that we want to work with, then we are able to split up the data in a random manner. This is why we would want to work with cross-validation. With this one, each day is going to be part of our test data, and then we would need to consider the data that we worked with from the day before as some of our training set.

a. A good place to start with this one is by training out the model on the minimum amount of observations and then we will be able to focus on this data and using it for the next day to help us test the data. And then we will keep moving through the days like this in order to help the algorithm to learn ore. This is going to make it easier for us to consider the aspect of the time-series that will come up with this kind of prediction.

The Hyperparameter Optimization

The next thing that we need to take a closer look at when we are working with our optimization is the idea of the hyperparameters. These are going to be important because they are properties that are specific to the model that we want to work with, ones that will be fixed before we really have a chance to test or train the data that we have with this model. Before we spend too much time trying to get through all of this though, we have to take a look at some of the optimization of this that we talked about earlier, because this is going to make it easier for us to handle some of what we talk about here.

A good way to take a look at the idea of a hyperparameter optimization is to look at the random forest. This hyperparameter is going to help us out because it will tell us how many decision trees we are going to have in the random forest that you are working with. When we want to handle one of the neural networks, we will find that there is going to be a rate of learning, the layers that are going to be hidden, the number of units that you would like to show up in all of these layers, and even the types of parameters that we are focusing on as well.

While we are able to bring up the topic of tuning our hyperparameter, we are going to not look at something that is outside of searching for the hyperparameters that we are able to use to make sure we get the high accuracy and precision that we are looking for. When we are ready to optimize these parameters, we will end up with one of the hardest parts of the whole process that we need to handle here. But it is so important to helping us to get things done as well.

The main aim that we will get when using this is that we want to find the sweet spot along the way. This is going to be the sweet spot of the model and will be the most important because it allows us to get the best performance on the projects that we do possible. The neat thing with this one though is that we are able to find a few techniques that will make life easier for parameter tuning, but the two most important ones and the ones that we are going to spend our time on the most here will be the random search and the grid search.

Random and Grid Search

And the last thing that we are going to look at when we work with this chapter is how the grid search and the random search are going to work in comparison to one another. This is important because it helps a program to figure out which out of these two is going to be the best for the work and results that we want to see. Before we dive too much into this one, we have to review some of the hyperparameter optimizations and see how this is going to fit into this kind of section as well.

First, our goal is to learn more about a process that is known as grid searching. This is where we are going to go through and try out all of the combinations of a list that we have to those hyperparameters, and then we will be able to evaluate each of these combinations to see what will happen. The pattern that we then choose to work with here is going to be similar to what we are able to see on the grid from before, but this is because the values will be placed into a kind of matrix to sort them out.

When the matrix is being set, we will be able to set up all of our parameters so that we can look them over and take them into consideration, taking a note at how accurate each one is going to be. Once all of these can be evaluated on their own the model that has the most accurate parameters out of all our choices will be the right one that we want to work with.

There are going to be times when we will decide that it is best to work with the method known as the grid search. But while this is a good option to work with, sometimes it is going to be too complex and too long to work with. This is where we are going to switch our work over to a random search. This is going to be a good technique where some of the random combinations of the hyperparameter that we use to help us figure out the best solution for the model that we are able to build up.

There are going to be many cases when this search is going to help us to look through the information and can help us try out a few of the combinations that may seem random for the range of values that we have. To help us to optimize this kind of random search though, the function will need to go through an evaluation at some of the random configurations of the parameter space along with the other work.

The chances that we have of finding the parameter that is the most optimal for our needs are going to increase when we work with the random search. This is because the pattern is going to be rained on in the optimized parameters, and we will not need to know some of the aliases ahead of time. Then the random search is going to be able to work the best when we are working with some of the data that is considered lower-dimensional data because the time that will be taken to help us find the right set for this is going to be lower when you don't need to go through as many iterations to get it done.

We will find here that the random search is going to be one of the best techniques out of the two that we are able to work with, especially when the number of dimensions that we need to focus on is lower. There are a lot of concerns, both theoretical and practical, that we need to work with when we evaluate these strategies. And the strategy that ends up being the best for the particular problem that we are working with is going to always be the one that is able to find the best value that we can work with, without having to go through as many evaluations.

Keep in mind when we are going through with this one is that the grid search is sometimes seen as a machine learning algorithm that is less common. This is why we are more likely to work with the random search to get the work done. This random search is able to get us the same, and often better, values when we compare it over to the grid search, and we won't have to go through as many evaluations of the functions for some of the problems that we want to be able to work with as well. Of course, though, we need to decide which method is going to be the best for some of the work that we would like to do in the process as well.

Chapter 12: Other Algorithms That Work Well with Python Machine Learning

Before we are done with this guidebook and all that we are able to learn from it along the way, it is time for us to take a look at just a few more of the algorithms that we are able to use when it comes to Python and machine learning working together. You will find that there are endless amounts of machine learning algorithms that we are able to work with when it is time to handle data science or some of the other cool things that you are able to do with machine learning. And often you are only limited by what you would like to do with the information and any challenges that you may face along the way. With this in mind, some of the different algorithms that you are able to use, that we have not discussed in this guidebook yet, will include:

Naïve Bayes

The first option that we are going to spend some time on here is going to be the Naïve Bayes algorithm. To get a better understanding of how we are able to make sure that this one works, we will need to imagine something for a moment. Let's start out by pretending that we are doing some new project, and it comes with a few challenges of classification along the way. At the same time, we are looking at these challenges and we want to figure out which hypothesis is going to work out the best for this. Then there is the problem of figuring out a design that is good because you want to add in the right features and discussions based on how important all of the variables are to the model.

This is a lot of things that we need to try and balance about our project to make sure that it is going to work the way that we want, and it may seem like a tall order for just one of the algorithms that we have. But the Naïve Bayes is able to help us get it done. Once we have been able to go through and gather up the information that we need, you will also find that there will be shareholders in the company, or at least some important investors, who are interested in seeing a model of what you plan to do.

This may seem hard to do. All you have right now is the data and a little plan. But the shareholders and investors want to be able to go through and see what is going to happen and what they can expect, without waiting a long time for you to be able to get it all done to show them. And you want to make sure that you show that information in a manner that is easy to understand and doesn't use a ton of technical jargon along the way.

This is going to be a big dilemma for you as a programmer to start out with. First, when you are to this stage, the information that you are working with is not going to be done. And even if you had a better handle on the information here, you may think that it is too complex for another person to look at here. How are we able to make it all set up so that the investors can see what is going on, even though you are not done yet, but making one of these models isn't going to be easy, and you have to worry about how complete it as well, and that is a challenge that we have to learn how to handle.

Often, when we are working with the process of data analysis, you may end up with a model that has hundreds of thousands of points that you need to work with and show on the model. It is even possible that while you are doing some of the recommended training and testing that some new variables will show up that you have to consider as well. with all of this information going on around us and with us not being done with all of it, how are we able to really go through the information and then make sure it is in the format that is the easiest for us to understand along the way.

The good news with this one and the thing that we need to remember when we work with the Naïve Bayes is that it is one of the best algorithms to work with in order to help us really get through the beginning stages done and going. It is designed to help us to really present all of the different types of information that we need, while still making sure that it is simple enough that everyone is able to use, even those who are not data scientists will be able to understand what is going on and make sense of it all.

This model is a good one for the data scientist to put together as well. And since it is going to be used to help you get through some of the biggest sets of data in a way that is simplified, you will find that it is one of the best methods for us to use as well for this kind of situation. One of the advantages that we are going to see with this kind of model though is that it is simple, and that simplicity is going to make it one of the best options to use when you are getting started with some of the machine learning that you want to work with.

As you start to learn more about the Naïve Bayes algorithm, you may find that there are a ton of reasons why you would want to learn how to make this one work for some of your needs. For example, this is a good one to use because of its ease of use, and this is even more true for those who are beginners and who have never been able to work in machine learning or deep learning in the past.

You will then find that the Naïve Bayes algorithm is going to be an effective method to work with when it is time for us to make some predictions for the sets of data that we are using and which classes they should end up in. This is a good thing because it helps to keep things in the set of data as simple as possible. It does have a high-performance level though too, despite being one of the easier algorithms to learn, and it can often seem more sophisticated to work with than it may be.

While there are going to be a number of benefits that we are able to work with when it comes to handling the Naïve Bayes model, it is important to know that there are a few negatives as well, just like with any of the other algorithms that we can spend our time on. The first downfall of this algorithm is that when you work with an algorithm that is going to be set with categorical variables, you have to make sure that the data you are going through for the testing phase is not the same data that you used for training. This will then cause you to end up with predictions that are not that accurate, and then you have to rely on probability, which is not all that accurate either.

Markov Algorithm

Another option that we are able to take some time looking over is going to be known as the Markov algorithm. This one is going to fit under the umbrella of the unsupervised machine learning that we will want to do on some of our projects. This is a good algorithm for us to work with because it is going to help us gather up all of the data that we choose to place into it, and then it will translate it out so that it can work with the coding language of our choice. This may work with Python if that is the coding language that you want to focus on, but it is also going to work with other coding languages as well.

One of the reasons that a lot of programmers like to work with this algorithm is because it allows them to choose some of the rules that they are able to use ahead of time with this algorithm so that it takes on the direction that they wish. Many programmers like the Markov Algorithm because it helps them to come up with the rules, rather than them having to always follow the rules and trying to make the data fit into this. You can use this benefit in order to take a whole string of data and make sure that it is something useful for the job or the project that you are handling at the time.

The second thing that programmers often like with this kind of algorithm is that there are several methods that work with this one, rather than just one path. One option to consider here is that the algorithm is going to be something that a lot of programmers can use on projects like FNA. For example, you could use this algorithm on a sequence of DNA, and then use it to translate some of the information that is found inside of all that.

This is going to help us make things easier for a lot of o people including scientists, doctors, and programmers so that they can see what information is inside of the DNA and then make better predictions in the future as well. when you are working with a computer as a programmer, you will find that the DNA sequence is sometimes hard to go through and understand all that well, but it is often easier to look through and understand the numerical data, and this is where the Markov Algorithm is able to help.

You may also find that another reason to work with the Markov algorithm is that it is going to be good when you would like to learn about problems where you can put in the right input but you are a bit uncertain about the parameters. This algorithm is going to be able to find the insights that are inside of that information. There are some situations where these insights are going to be hidden, and it is going to be able to find some of these insights better than other algorithms can do in some situations.

Of course, while there are a lot of benefits that come with using this algorithm, there are also going to be some times when it may not be the best algorithm for your needs either. To start, the Markov algorithm is going to be a bit more difficult to work with compared to some of the other options out there. This is because you have to manually do the work any time you would like to create a new rule so that a second or third programming language can be used along with this algorithm.

If you only plan to use this algorithm with the Python language and never bring in another coding language along the way, then this is going to be something that you will not need to work with. But often your coding and the work that you want to do with machine learning will need more than one programming language to get it done, and if you end up needing to rewrite out the rules that you want in your codes a bunch of times, the process is going to get tedious.

Regression Algorithms

While you will find that there are many times when you can work with the Naïve Bayes algorithm to get your work done, there are times when it will not quite do the trick, and you may need to rely on something like the regression analysis. This is going to be the algorithm type that you will want to spend your time on if you are trying to see what relationship, if any, is there between the dependent variables and the predictor.

Programmers are going to be able to quickly find out that this is a technique that works well for them and they can use it in many situations where they need to be able to see if there is some kind of causal relationship between the forecasting that they see, with the various variables that they plan to work with, or even if they are working on the time series modeling that is in place.

The whole point of choosing this type of algorithm over some of the others is that it is going to be a good one to help you grab all of the information out of your data set and then get it to work, as closely as possible to one line or curve. Of course, depending on the data that you plan to use here, this line may not have as many points on it as you would like. But it is a good place for us to start, in a more visual form, to see if there are some similarities in the data that we are working with.

There are times when a company or a data scientist is going to choose to handle this kind of algorithm because it is a good one when we want to make predictions. The company will then take the predictions that come out of these regression algorithms in order to increase their profits overall in some manner. It is even possible to work with this kind of algorithm to make an estimate of how much the sales of a company can grow, while still having the ability to base it on how the economy and the conditions of this are doing at the time.

There are a lot of things that we are able to enjoy when it comes to the regression algorithm, but one thing that a lot of data scientists like with this one is that it has room for them to add in some of the pertinent information that they would like to use. You are able to go through and add in any information that you want if you think that it will help you to get a more accurate prediction as well. so, adding in information about how the economy is doing now, and how it was doing in the past, could be important and useful based on the data that you want to handle as well.

This is important here is that the regression algorithm is going to be used to help us figure out the most likely and the most profitable way that we will see some growth in our company in the future. But to make sure that this one works the way that we would need, we have to make sure that the company is putting in the right kind of data and information, or the predictions could come out wrong.

One example that we are able to see with this is if the company is trying to find the right algorithm of machine learning so that they can learn not just if their company is growing, but to see what rate the company is growing and if this is similar, faster, or slower compared to some of the other companies that they compete against. We can then use this information to make some predictions on how the company will do in the future and then they can make some changes if this is not up to their standards.

We will find that there is more than one algorithm that can be considered in the term regression, and you have to really know about your data and what you would like to accomplish with it, in order to figure out which of these algorithms is the best for you to choose. While there are a number of options that work well, some of the most common of these regression algorithms that your company may be able to benefit from includes:

1. Stepwise regression
2. Linear regression
3. Logistic regression
4. Polynomial regression
5. Ridge regression

As you can see here, working with the regression algorithm will be able to present us with a few different kinds of benefits if you choose to use it. To start out with, you will see that these are the algorithms that can make it easier for anyone using the information to check whether there is some kind of relationship present to work with at all, between the dependent and independent variables. This is also the algorithm to use in order to show what kind of impact is going to show up if you try to add in a new variable or change up to another kind of variable that is in the set of data if you want to experiment with what is there a bit.

We also have to look at some of the downsides that come with this method to get a full picture of what is there. There are a few issues that come up, and one of the biggest of these is that you will notice how the regression algorithms, due to their name, will not be able to help you out with the classification problems that you have. The reason that these two ideas do not work out is that the regression algorithm is more likely to overfit the data in many situations. So if you try to add in a lot of different constraints here, you will find that it doesn't take long before the process gets tedious and you can often find a better algorithm in order to help handle this kind of thing instead.

Q-Learning

Now it is time for us to end with a look at how we are able to do something with the reinforcement learning that we talked about earlier. There are a lot of times when we will want to work with that kind of machine learning, but you will find that some of the algorithms really are not as glamorous or well-known as we are used to seeing with some of the other options along the way. That is going to change here when we take a look at what we are able to do with this kind of learning algorithm.

With the Q-learning algorithm, we are going to work with any kind of project that wants to focus on something known as temporal difference learning. As we are working with machine learning, you will notice that this algorithm is more of an off-policy option. It is known in this manner because it is not going to have the ability to learn the action-value function in a manner similar to the other options of algorithms. Sometimes this is a good thing, and other times it could add some issues to the learning that you would like to work with.

Since this is going to be a useful option to a programmer because they are able to use it no matter the function they would like to create in the data set, it is still important for us to go through and learn a bit more about this method and what it is able to do for us. The learner needs to do this ahead of time because it is going to help them to pick out the course of action that is the best for them. Of course, keep in mind with this one that one of the drawbacks to using it is that it has a few more steps to get the model done compared to some of the other steps. But because it is going to be more efficient than the other models, and because it does work well, you may find that the time and the effort are well worth it in the long run.

After you have been able to go through with this algorithm and find the action-value function that will work the best for your data points, it is time for you to create what is going to be known as the optimal policy. How are we supposed to be able to construct this with the Q-learning algorithm? The best way to get started with this is to use the actions that you think will come in at the highest value, regardless of the state that has been chosen to do this one in.

Depending on the kind of data that you want to go through, and the results that you are hoping to get, there could be a number of great advantages that come with using the algorithm in machine learning for Q-learning. One of the benefits of this is that you won't have to go through all of the effort or the time that is needed to put in the models of the environment so that the system is able to compare the means. You will be able to compare a few, and often a lot, of actions together and compare how they are going to be together. In addition, you can use any kind of environment that you would like to with this one, and still get the same results and be able to make the predictions that you would like.

You will find though that there are a few negatives that are likely when we work with this kind of reinforcement learning. We have to focus on how the main issue is that we will have to take on more steps to ensure this learning is going to happen. This process, because you do need to go through and write out the rules that you want to use and the course of action that will make the most sense to reach your goals, will provide us with more steps compared to a few of the other options. For those programmers who are in a hurry to be done, and who don't really care as much about the rules they put in place, this may not be the best option to choose.

As we can see from this kind of machine learning algorithm, and some of the many others that we have been able to explore in this guidebook, there are a lot of options when it is time to work with machine learning and getting the data sorted through and understandable in no time. There is no right or wrong algorithm that we are able to choose from. It is more about making sure that we go with the option that is right for our situation. This changes based on the situation, the data we have, the solution that we want, and so much more, but learning what this is and how we are able to use it to our advantage is going to help as well. All of these algorithms are great, and it is more about finding the one that is right for us, rather than choosing the one that is right or wrong all of the time.

Conclusion

Thank you for making it through to the end of *Learn Python*. Let's hope it was informative and able to provide you with all of the tools you need to achieve your goals whatever they may be.

The next step is to spend some time learning more about some of these amazing options in algorithms and more that you are able to focus on when it comes to handling machine learning and the Python language. When it comes to using Python and finally being able to really learn about the data that you have, and all of the different benefits that come with data science, you will find that this is the exciting part of the process. It is the part where we can actually take all of the data that we have and put it through the algorithm, finally getting the insights and the predictions that we are looking for.

And this is where we are going to spend some of our time exploring this guidebook as well. This guidebook is going to spend most of its time taking a look at some of the best algorithms that you are able to use when it comes to working on machine learning, especially when it comes to Python, and this can help you to really figure out which one is going to be the best for your own work with the data. You may be surprised by how many options there are when it comes to algorithms though, which is why we are going to spend some of our time looking through them and going through them in more detail.

In addition to learning about the benefits of working with Python and why this is often the most chosen out of all the languages when it is time to handle machine learning and some of its various algorithms for data science, we are going to really take a closer look at some of the great algorithms that we would want to use in this situation. Whether you are looking to create an algorithm that is for supervised, unsupervised, or reinforcement learning, we spent some time talking about how to use each one, when they are all going to be beneficial for your needs, and so much more.

Working with machine learning is a really great experience. There are going to be so many times when we are able to bring this up, and each industry, no matter what they work with or how they serve the customer, will be able to enjoy some of the benefits of machine learning. The more that it is used in our modern world, the more that we will be able to discover it and use it in the future. This is something that can be really exciting when it is time to work with machine learning. The algorithms that we are going to explore inside will help us to utilize this to its full potential.

There are so many times when we will want to work with machine learning, Python, and some of the machine learning algorithms that are explored in this guidebook. When we are ready to start learning more about these topics and how we are able to work with this process, or even if you are ready to use it for some of your own data science needs, make sure to check out this guidebook to see the steps that are needed to get started.

Finally, if you found this book useful in any way, a review on Amazon is always appreciated!

www.ingramcontent.com/pod-product-compliance
Lightning Source LLC
Chambersburg PA
CBHW071140050326
40690CB00008B/1515